Simply
MAP-READING

Ordnance Survey

Telegraph
— MAPS

Simply
MAP-READING
RICHARD NEVE

First published 1988
   by Telegraph Publications
Peterborough Court, At South Quay
181 Marsh Wall, London E14 9SR
   and Ordnance Survey
Romsey Road, Maybush
Southampton, SO9 4DH

Coordinated by Michael Nyman, Pamino Publications

Typeset by DP Photosetting, Aylesbury Bucks
Printed by Jerez Industrial, SA, Spain

British Library Cataloguing in Publication Data

Neve, Richard
   Simply map reading.
   1. Map reading – Manuals
   I. Title
   912'.01'4

   ISBN 0-86367-286-8
   Ordnance Survey ISBN 0 319 001 539

CONTENTS

PREFACE

Never travel without a map. By using one, you will get so much more out of your journey.

Not only does a map save you time by helping you keep to your chosen route, it also enables you to appreciate fully the area through which you are travelling. Knowing for certain what to expect round the corner turns a simple journey into an exciting expedition.

This short book is based on the knowledge the author has gained over many years of map-reading. He is proud to claim: 'I have never once got lost; temporarily unsure of my position, yes, but lost – never!' This book tells you how to become equally confident.

Other books are concerned with the theory and geography of maps: useful if you are studying them at an academic level but only marginally helpful if you need a map just to get from A to B. Here you will find nothing but practical advice on using a map to find your way.

Yes, you do have to concentrate on both the map and the ground, but the effort of concentration will not stop you enjoying the journey. On the contrary, it will increase enjoyment by helping you to appreciate and exploit the map-maker's skill as you go along.

There are four easy rules to learn and there is an art in knowing how to keep to them. But once you have mastered that art, not only will you be certain to arrive quickly and surely at your destination, you will also know exactly where you are at all times on the way. On the other hand, if you are not sure where you are, you are certain to have broken one of the rules.

A novice will find here all that is needed to set off confidently with map and compass in hand. Even experienced map-readers will discover some useful tips and, in particular, find the book an asset when passing on the art to others. There are also special sections for motorists and group leaders.

INTRODUCTION

The four simple rules of map reading are:

1. Know exactly where you started from.
2. Always check direction on moving off and whenever you change it.
3. Remember the scale.
4. Read ahead.

Rule 1 is so important it stands alone. In order to keep to it you have to be able to interpret correctly all the signs and other marks printed on the map. This will enable you to visualise in your mind's eye the ground as it will be when you cross it.

The other three rules are subordinate to Rule 1 but, taken together, they will keep you on your route.

Although it is quite possible to read a map without a compass it is much easier and safer if you use one to keep to Rule 2. Who knows when fog will descend or an accident will force you to change your route to one where a compass is essential?

Before we examine in detail what you have to do to stick to the rules, we must look first at how to use your two basic tools, the map and compass.

THE TOOLS

THE MAP

Slingsby, N. Yorkshire

From an aeroplane you have a bird's eye view of the land below. This photograph shows what you would see over a typical English village: very interesting it is too. But what is the name of the village? Which county is it in? Where is the parish boundary? Where do the roads lead to? How high is it above sea level? What is the distance from the crossroads at the bottom of the picture to what looks like a sports field at the top? Is it a sports field? Which paths are rights of way? How can you accurately refer to a particular spot on the ground?

All this information can be found on a map. Nevertheless, even without all this information, if you knew you were somewhere within the area shown on the photograph, without too much

9

difficulty you could probably use the photograph to find your way around the village with considerable accuracy.

However, now look at the shot below of some typical moorland. You would find it very difficult indeed to identify where you are on the photograph. Even if you knew, it would be almost impossible to find your way across country using only this photograph, especially if it was foggy.

What is a Map?

A map is a sheet of paper or card on which features on the ground are represented by means of conventional signs. These bear the same relationship to one another for distance, direction and height above sea level as they do on the ground.

Conventional Signs

The conventional signs used on a map are normally printed in the margins or on the cover of the map. It is important that you should know them well enough to be able to recognise them instantly. They are not difficult to learn as nearly all of them have some feature connecting them to the object they represent.

Some conventional signs used, for example, on the Ordnance Survey 1:50 000 Landranger Series are detailed opposite.

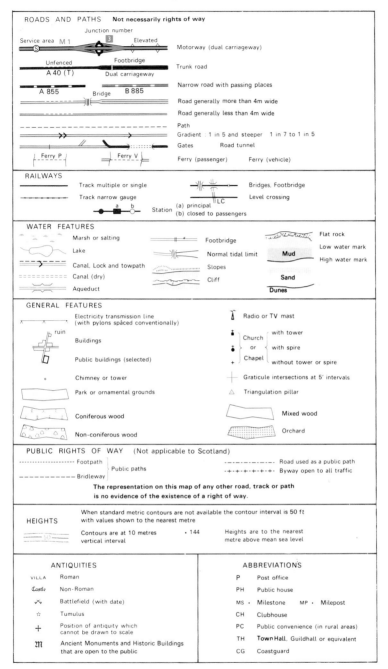

It is important to note the following points about some key conventional signs on Ordnance Survey 1:50 000 Landranger maps.

Roads

Fenced roads are bordered with a continuous line, unfenced roads by a broken line.

Fenced   Unfenced

Power Lines

On the symbol for power lines, the pylons are spaced conventionally, not where they stand on the ground.

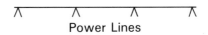

Power Lines

Tall Features

For tall features such as churches, radio or TV masts and windmills the base of the sign marks the position on the ground.

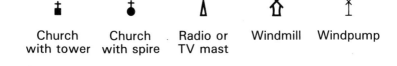

Church   Church   Radio or   Windmill   Windpump
with tower   with spire   TV mast

Public Rights of Way and Paths

Paths which are public rights of way are shown in red. Other paths for which there is no evidence of a right of way are shown in black.

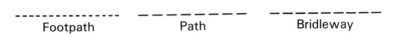

Footpath   Path   Bridleway

Water Features

The banks of a river are marked in black up to the highest point to which tides normally flow.

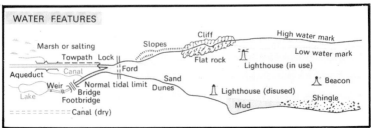

Trees

Note the difference between:

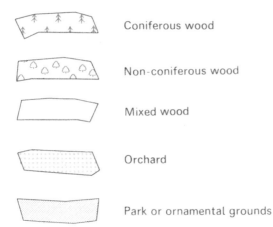

Coniferous wood

Non-coniferous wood

Mixed wood

Orchard

Park or ornamental grounds

As with roads, if the boundary of the feature is unfenced or indeterminate it is shown by a broken line.

MAKING A MAP

Let us use some of these conventional signs to make a small map of our own.

Start with a square on a plain sheet of paper to indicate the extent of the map then mark a blue line to represent a stream running across it:

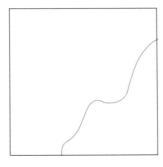

Apart from the fact that the stream changes direction slightly, we can tell very little from the information we have so far. We do not know if the stream is flowing from the top to the bottom of the map or vice versa. As it is customary to print all maps with north at the top we can probably say it runs either roughly north to south or south to north.

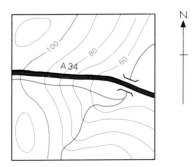

So we can now add a North point in the margin. However to show the direction of flow of the river we need to add information on the lie of the land. We can do this by means of lines linking points of the same height known as contours (page 22). Armed with this information we can now see that the river flows northwards from the high ground to the south and is joined by a tributary flowing in from the hills to the west. A road following the valley of the tributary crosses the main river just north of their confluence. The picture of the area is now building up but what we still do not know is the distance on the ground that is represented by our map. For this we need a scale.

SCALE

The scale of your map is the first thing you should look for. Without this information you will not be able to get the most from your map. The scale is the relationship between distances measured on the ground and the same distances represented on the map. It is normally expressed as a ratio such as 1:50 000 but for convenience it is also described in easily visualised units such as 2 centimetres to 1 kilometre or 1 ¼ inches to 1 mile. Because of its importance this information is usually shown in a prominent position on the map cover, or in the margin of the map sheet. The following example is taken from an Ordnance Survey (OS) 1:50 000 map sheet.

SCALE 1:50 000

Scale Descriptions

When scale is referred to as a ratio such as 1:50 000 this means that 1 unit of measurement on the map is equivalent to 50,000 units of measurement on the ground. Ratio values can be given in either metric or imperial measures provided they are applied uniformly to both map and ground measurements.

Therefore for 1:50 000 scale maps:

1 inch on the map is equivalent to 50,000 inches on the ground.
1 centimetre on the map is equivalent to 50,000 centimetres on the ground.

Map scales expressed in units of measurement mean the same thing but are more easily envisaged. For example, Ordnance Survey 1:50 000 scale maps are also described as 2 centimetres to 1 kilometre or $1\frac{1}{4}$ inches to 1 mile on the basis that:

Metric

If 100,000 centimetres = 1 kilometre,
and 1 centimetre on the map = 50,000 centimetres on the ground,
then 2 centimetres on the map = 1 kilometre on the ground.

Imperial

If 63,360 inches = 1 mile,
and 1 inch on the map = 50,000 inches on the ground,
then $1\frac{1}{4}$ inches (1.267) on the map = 1 mile on the ground.

Maps are also referred to as large or small scale. These are relative terms but to compare scale sizes try to remember the following. Across the maps to be compared, look at the distances on the ground which are represented by the same units of measurement on each map. You will see that the smaller the ground distance covered the larger the map scale. Therefore 1:25 000 maps where 1 unit of measurement on the map equals 25,000 units of measurement on the ground are at a larger scale than 1:50 000 maps where 1 unit of measurement on the map equals 50,000 units of measurement on the ground.

Another way of coming to the same conclusion is to remember that 50,000 units on the ground require only 1 map unit on 1:50 000 maps but need 2 map units on 1:25 000 maps.

15

Map extracts below demonstrate these relative scale sizes. Look particularly at the depiction of the driveway to Blenheim Palace which has been highlighted.

Practical Use of Scales

For practical purposes it is a good idea to get fixed in your mind the distance on the map that represents a convenient distance on the ground.

On foot, a distance of 100 metres is recommended. Thus, when you are using a 1:50000 scale map, 100 metres on the ground is represented by 2 millimetres on the map.

On a 1:25000 scale map, 100 metres on the ground is represented by 4 millimetres on the map.

Of these two scales, the 1:25000 particularly is ideal for walking. (Ordnance Survey Landranger and Pathfinder map series respectively cover the country at these scales.)

In the car, a mile or kilometre is a more convenient distance to use. At 1:50000 scale, 1 kilometre on the ground is represented by 2 centimetres (20 millimetres) on the map, whilst 1 mile on the ground is represented by $1\frac{1}{4}$ inches on the map.

This is probably the largest practical scale of mapping to use in a car. Anything larger will mean you need a lot of map sheets to cover even a relatively short journey. An even smaller scale map may be better such as 1:250000 where 1 kilometre on the ground is represented by 4 millimetres on the map and 1 mile on the ground is represented by $\frac{1}{4}$ inch on the map. Ordnance Survey Routemaster maps, which cover the whole country, are at this scale.

These map extracts show the area around Blenheim Palace at three different scales:

1:250000

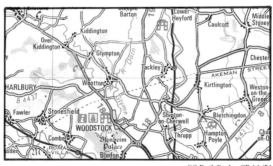

OS Pathfinder SP 41/51

1:50 000

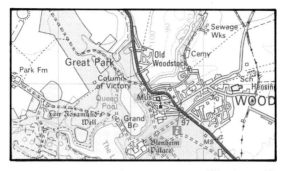

OS Landranger 164

1:25 000

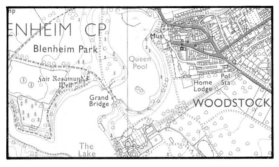

OS Routemaster 9

We can use the scale to calculate the distance between the forecourt on the north east side of the Palace straight along the drive to the gate. There are a number of ways of doing this. The simplest is to judge it by eye. It is usually quite accurate enough for the traveller.

If you need to be more accurate, take a straight edge (a sheet of paper is easiest) lay it between the two points making a mark at each, transfer it to the scale and read off the distance. If you do not have paper and pencil, use a blade of grass, matchstick or twig; break it off to fit the distance and place it on the scale. You can lay them on the map like a ruler to measure distances.

The answer is 1,400 metres. But you will see that the most accurate measure is only obtainable at the 1:25 000 or largest scale.

If you want to measure along a twisting route, the simplest way is to use one of these methods and then make an allowance for the bends. But if you have to be more accurate then mark off each section of the route along a sheet of paper, turning it to fit as you go, then read it off on the scale. Alternatively you can lay a piece

17

of string or thread carefully along the route and then measure it. It is all rather fiddly and worth doing only if it is essential to be accurate.

GRID REFERENCES

In the map extracts on pages 16 and 17 it was easy to refer to the palace and gate-house by describing them as they were the only ones marked on the map. Of course the normal map has many identical features marked on it to which we might need to refer, or we may need to refer to a spot in the middle of a field. With a map this is easy: we use a Grid Reference.

The Ordnance Survey National Grid is a reference system of squares which have been overprinted on Ordnance Survey maps since the 1940s. This system of breaking the country down into squares allows you to pinpoint any place in the country with varying levels of precision depending on the scale of map you are using. For example on a 1:50000 scale map (2 centimetres to 1 kilometre; 1¼ inches to 1 mile) you can give a reference to an accuracy of 100 metres (333.3 feet).

The National Grid reference for a place or feature is unique and will always be the same no matter which map or scale you are using. But it must be stressed that to ensure the 'uniqueness' of the reference the National Grid letters as well as numbers must always be included.

The basis of the National Grid is a series of 100 kilometre grid squares which cover the whole of Great Britain. Each of these squares is identified by two letters as shown on the diagram opposite. Square SK has been highlighted. Information on the relevant 100 kilometre grid squares covered by a specific Ordnance Survey map is always included in that map's legend.

UNDERSTANDING THE GRID

Each 100 kilometre grid square is subdivided into smaller squares. In the case of the Ordnance Survey 1:50000 and 1:25000 scale maps, the smaller grid squares cover an area of 1 × 1 kilometre. They are defined on the map by grid lines, each line being identified by a two-figure number. The grid lines are numbered from 01 in an easterly (left to right) and northerly (upward) direction from the South West (bottom left) corner of each 100 kilometre grid square. The easterly grid lines are known as Eastings and northerly grid lines as Northings.

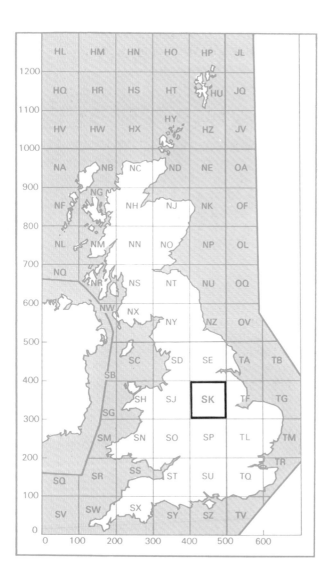

If we extract the highlighted square SK, we can look at it more closely. The shaded square in the diagram overleaf can be identified as SK 7458. This is the reference for the south-west corner of that square and is constructed as follows:

SK = the reference for the 100 kilometre square in which the shaded area falls.

7458 = the number of the easterly (Eastings) grid line followed by the northerly (Northings) grid line which intersect to give the south-west corner of the square.

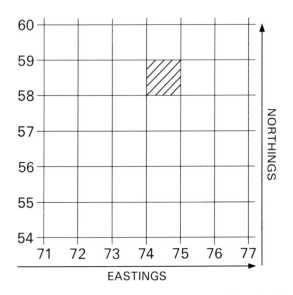

When constructing a grid reference, always give the Eastings number before the Northings and if you have trouble remembering say 'along the hall *then* up the stairs'.

The four-figure reference given above identifies the location of a feature to within 1 kilometre. To pinpoint a place to 100 metres within the 1 kilometre grid square, we can mentally subdivide the square into ten (in line with the following diagram) and give a six figure grid reference.

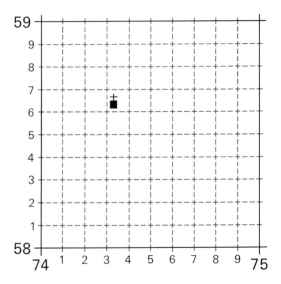

Therefore the church symbolised in this diagram has a reference SK 743586 on the basis that:

SK = the reference of the 100 kilometre grid square in which the shaded area falls.

74 = The Eastings grid line number

58 = The Northings grid line number

These together define the 1 kilometre grid square in which the church lies.

The remaining figures in the reference (74**3** 58**6**) identify the imaginary lines which pinpoint the feature within that square, again following the principle of quoting Eastings before Northings. Use this system to find on the map below:

The church at SK 568 970
The mine at SK 545 991
Cockhill Farm at SK 546 962

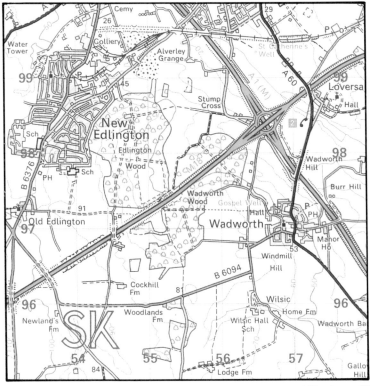

OS Landranger 111

Points to remember on Grid References:

* For a unique reference always quote the 100 kilometre square reference letters.

* Eastings before Northings 'along the hall *then* up the stairs.'

* If you are working out a six-figure grid reference by eye, it is easier to divide the grid square in half mentally (the eye does this naturally) and then divide the half into five parts, rather than try to work directly in tenths.

* One tenth of a grid square on Ordnance Survey 1:50 000 and 1:25 000 scale maps represents 100 metres on the ground. You should try and get this distance fixed in your mind's eye as it will help you keep a track on your progress.

CONTOURS

If the most important attribute of a successful map-reader is to be able to visualise distance instantly by knowledge of the scale, then close behind that comes the ability to visualise the shape of the ground by a quick glance at the marks on the paper. We do this by means of the orange or brown lines known as contour lines.

At any point on a contour line you are always at the same height above sea level.

Look at the illustration below. The top half of the figure is a section of a hill. Imagine a giant has carved it into slices each 50 feet thick, put each slice one by one on the ground and drawn a line round the bottom edge, and you get the plan in the lower picture. Note carefully and remember that where the contour lines are close together the slope is steep, where they are further apart it is more gradual.

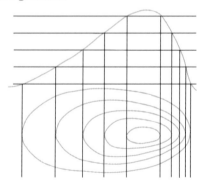

It is useful to be able to recognise the following features at a glance by their characteristic pattern of contour lines.

Spur   Valley   Saddle

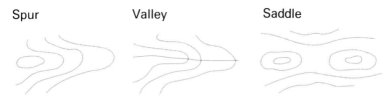

A concave slope is illustrated below. Note that the contour lines are closer together, therefore the ground is steeper at the top. When standing at the base of this type of slope, you can see all the ground from top to bottom and vice versa from the summit.

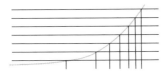

In the convex slope, the contour lines are closer together and the ground steeper at the bottom. You cannot see all the ground from top to bottom either from base or summit.

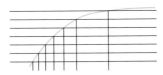

It is also important to realise that it is possible for a hillock to be up to 49 feet high and not show on the map:

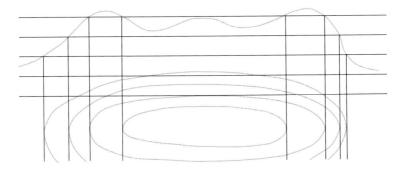

Where the ground slopes very gently, and there are no streams to guide you, it can sometimes be difficult to tell which is the uphill side of a contour line. In this case it is useful to know that the figures on a contour line are always printed with the top of the numbers facing uphill:

The distance between contours on the map is known as the contour interval. On the older 1:50000 scale maps it is 50 feet but this is being converted to 10 metres (about 32 feet) on new editions. Conversion should be completed by 1990. If you need to check, the contour interval is stated in the information in the margins of the map but it is usually only necessary to glance at the contour lines on the map to see from the figures on them what the interval is. You should note that every fifth contour line is thicker than the others. So thick ones are 250 feet (about 76 metres) apart on the older maps and 50 metres apart on the new ones.

As well as contour lines, height information is also shown on Ordnance Survey 1:50000 maps by means of spot heights. These show heights to the nearest metre above mean sea level. The following extract contains spot height examples (eg .156).

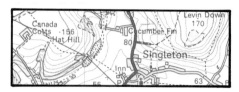

OS Landranger 197

THE COMPASS

The Lanyard

The most important part of a compass is the lanyard that fastens it to you. It could save your life if it prevents you from losing your compass. It is all too easy to drop a loose compass if you fall or are tired, wet, cold and hungry at the end of a long day. How you fasten the lanyard to you is a matter of personal preference. It can be secured round your neck, through an epaulette or to your belt. I prefer the last method.

The Compass Pouch

You will need to check your direction on your compass at frequent intervals. You will be less inclined to do so if you have to dig deep into a pocket or pouch every time. It is best to keep your compass in its own pouch where it is easy to reach and cannot get muddled with anything else. This pouch should be fastened to your belt just forward of your hip. It should have a flip top and be stiffened so that the compass can easily be slipped in and out.

North

I assume that everyone knows that a compass points to the north. Most know that it points to magnetic north which is not the same as true north. If you have done some map-reading before or have studied the margins of the map carefully you probably know that the vertical grid lines on a map point to grid north and that this is different again. Some may have learned how to convert a grid bearing to a magnetic bearing. You can forget all that. If you follow the rules in this book you are most unlikely to need to draw bearings on maps and do sums to find your position.

In the mid-1980s the magnetic variation in Great Britain was around 5 degrees. Even if you make an error of 5 degrees over a distance of one kilometre you will at most be 87 metres off course. But it is more likely that over that distance there will be features marked on the map from which to check your position as you progress. Also, unless the ground is particularly flat and featureless it is most unlikely you will walk in a dead straight line along a bearing. If you are sensible you will keep to an overall direction, but pick the easiest going that keeps you close to your course. Here we see how magnetic variation is shown on 1:50000 Ordnance Survey map number 170.

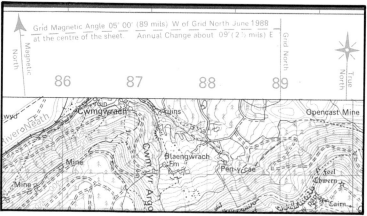

Bearings

Only a map-reader who lacks confidence will set a bearing and plough in a dead straight line over hill and dale. It may occasionally be necessary to set and to follow accurately a bearing on a compass: the following illustrations will tell you how to do so. But normally all you need to do is take a quick glance at the compass to see that you are going in the right general direction. You then use the features on the ground to check your accurate position.

The two main uses of the compass are to check the direction in which you are moving and to set the map. However before you can understand how to do these things you must know about the points of the compass.

Remember that a compass is affected by any metal containing iron – even certain cameras may affect it. It is therefore a wise precaution to check your compass against any metal object you are wearing. Do not use it in or near a vehicle, electric pylon or other magnetic metal object. Most buckles and badges are made of alloy these days but if yours are magnetic remember to hold the compass at arm's length when using it.

Setting the Map

To set a map is to turn it so that the features on the ground are in the same direction on the map as they are on the ground: so that north on the map is in the same direction as north on the ground.

Why is it necessary to set a map? Because it makes it so much easier to identify features when they are all in the same relative position on the map and on the ground.

One of the most common causes of map-reading errors is failure to carry out this simple act. You should do this not only at the start of the journey but you should keep the map properly set throughout the trip.

Features on the map are marked by symbols which are easy to read whichever way they are turned. Most people can read one or two words of print upside down. But if you find it difficult to read place names the wrong way up by all means turn it the right way up to read, but TURN IT BACK AGAIN IMMEDIATELY you have finished.

Using the Compass

To check that you have got the idea, imagine you have just emerged from the wood at SU855150 on the following map extract, taken from Landranger Series, Sheet 197.

26

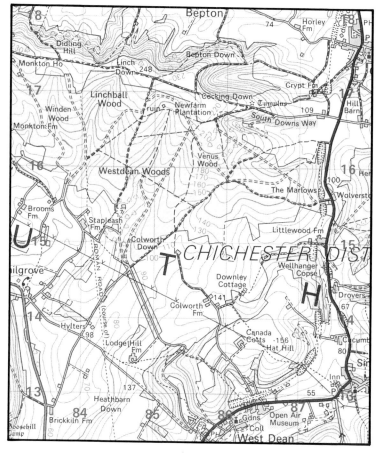

OS Landranger 197

You can see at a quick glance that the corner of the wood to the due east is about 300 metres away, the farm in the lower ground to your south-west is also about 300 metres away, and the point due north-west where the bridle paths meet as they go into the wood is about 250 metres away as it should be. If they did not all fit you would not be at X.

There is no need to transfer the compass directions, or bearings as they are known, to your map by drawing lines all over it; you are not a surveyor, you just want to get from A to B by your chosen route.

That was an easy one. Now let us try something a bit more difficult. On the map extract overleaf you are moving due north up the footpath where it leaves the lane at (1). The footpath is not much used and difficult to distinguish from a number of sheep tracks in the area so after going about 1,700 metres you

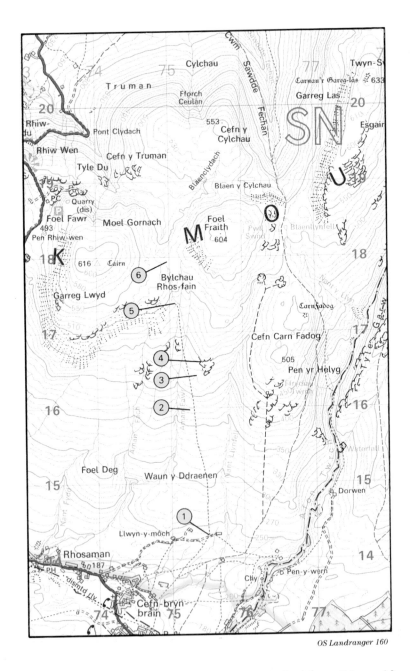

OS Landranger 160

decide to check your position. As you cross the 16 northing grid line (you will not find it on the ground!) if you look carefully at the map you will see that there is a bend in the contour line to the west of the footpath. This means that at that point there will be a slight rise or spur to your immediate left. After you have climbed another 40 metres to the 420 metre contour line you should be able to identify the indentation (3) due west of the base of the rocky outcrop (4). When you reach the end of the footpath (5) you will probably pick the easiest route up to the saddle (6) where there should be no problem in checking your position for the next leg of your journey. The trick is to learn to look at the minute detail on the map in your immediate vicinity and use it to fix your exact position.

The point of all that was to demonstrate that you do not have to be able to see church spires, roads or edges of woods to locate your position. All you need is a properly set map, a couple of natural features and some contour lines. This particular extract is taken from the 1:50 000 Landranger Series Sheet 160 Brecon Beacons.

The Silva Compass

One of the most common and reliable types of compass carried when travelling is the Silva compass. It is light, strong and simple to use.

1. Just place the compass on the map with one edge or engraved line along your route.

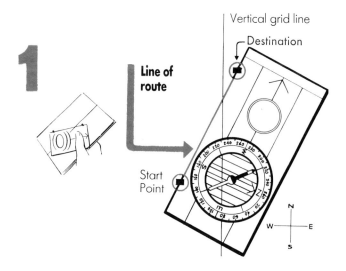

2. With the compass on the map, turn the dial until the lines engraved in it are parallel with the vertical grid lines on the map. North on the dial will then point to north on the map.

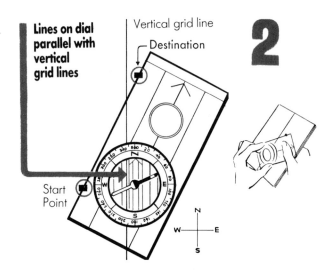

Lines on dial parallel with vertical grid lines

Vertical grid line

Destination

Start Point

3. Remove the compass from the map, hold it flat and turn it so that the red needle points to north on the dial. Do not change the dial setting.

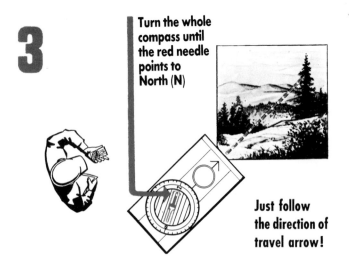

Turn the whole compass until the red needle points to North (N)

Just follow the direction of travel arrow!

4. Then just follow the direction of travel arrow and you will be on course.

THE RULES

RULE 1. Know exactly where you started from

You must know exactly where you start your journey. Not just at the beginning of the journey but each time you restart after a halt. It is important to be 100% certain. Nine times out of 10 it is easy, but if you are not sure it is well worth taking time to check. Choose an easily identifiable point to start from. Comparatively featureless woods and hills give the biggest problems.

Is the track you propose to take through the wood the one marked on the map? In recently planted areas it may well not be. The old track may have become overgrown and been replaced by a new one, in which case, change your plans and take the new one. The important thing is to know what you are doing and why.

Before setting off over hilly country, perhaps along a ridge, check that it is the right one. Does it run in the correct direction? Is it the right height compared with those on either side? Is it the right distance from them? Everything must fit. If it does not, check and recheck until you are certain.

It is well worth ten minutes' delay to save three hours getting back on course, not to mention the energy you save and the party's confidence in your ability as a leader if you are in charge. Climb to a viewpoint and check directions on you compass. Go round the corner in the road to check that the road junction marked on the map is really there and that you have not stopped in the wrong place. Remember again, everything most fit, not just one or two things.

RULE 2. Always check direction on moving off and whenever you change it

Get the compass habit. Never move off without checking your direction on your compass. Check again every time you change direction.

Of course you will not bother to do this if you are following a well defined feature such as a road or track. Just check when you get to junctions to verify the track you want to take is the one marked on the map. But on ridges where visibility is limited, it is only too easy to veer off down a spur instead of sticking to the main ridge. If you do not notice it straightaway you can be faced with a stiff climb back to the right one. This can be demoralising when you are weary and looking forward to getting to shelter for the night. Most silly mistakes occur through tiredness and forgetting to check direction.

In open country you will not need to check so frequently as in close country. Pick a feature some way ahead and make for it. In very close country you may need to have your compass out all the time. Do not plough straight ahead through every bush and thicket; that is far too exhausting. Choose the easiest route and divert to left or right as the going dictates, but keep to the overall direction as closely as you can.

Very often when out in the country you will come across a track made by animals that is not marked on the map. Animals are just like us in that they do not choose to cross 20 feet deep ravines, go through bogs, climb over fallen trees, or force their way through thickets unless they have to. They take the easy route. Where the going ahead is difficult, a path will often appear where all the animals and people that pass that way have trodden the same route to avoid the obstacle. Do not be afraid to follow such paths, even if they appear to go up to 90 degrees off course, just check your compass, and press on. Nine times out of ten you will find the path veers back on course again after you have skirted an obstacle that would take considerable extra time and effort to surmount. The tenth time, because you have checked the compass, it is a simple matter to get back on course again.

RULE 3. Remember the scale

In many ways this is the most difficult rule to follow as it does require quite a lot of concentration to keep to it. To remember the scale correctly it is important to have a clear mental picture of the distance on the map that represents 100 metres on the ground. It is equally important to remember how many 100 metres you have travelled on the ground! And there are so many distractions. You know where you started. You know in which directions you have travelled. If you know the distance you have been, then you must have a good idea of exactly where you are.

If you are not on your own it is sometimes helpful if you ask your companion to keep a check on the distance. Over long legs of a trip, or in difficult country or when visibility is bad through mist or fog, it is best not to rely on memory. The average person covers 100 metres in about 120 paces on normal going. During a tiring slog up a long slope with the end not yet in sight it is all too easy to forget if you have travelled 1,200 or 1,300 metres. To keep track of the 100 metre count you can break off a piece of twig and put it in your pocket. Easy if there are plenty of twigs about but it is quite easy to drop one or lose it in the depths of your pocket. Alternatively you can have ten small pebbles in your pocket and transfer one from one pocket to another every 100 metres.

As you gain experience you will find that you get much better at estimating the distance you have travelled, probably by comparing the time you have been going with the speed you have been travelling. Of course you will only have to remember the distance until you reach the next point on the map at which you can be certain of your position. Then you start again, which brings us to our final rule.

RULE 4. Read ahead

To be a good map-reader the essential secret is to read ahead from your present position to the next mark on the map (but not grid lines) so that you can anticipate the next check point on your route. This is such a simple rule, but the one most frequently ignored due to lack of concentration!

If, as I hope you will, you come to appreciate the satisfaction to be gained from consistently accurate map-reading, you will soon begin to take pleasure in identifying the next mark on the map and then coming across the feature it represents exactly where it should be. You know you are on course. It will not happen if you just wander along with your mind in neutral.

But a word of warning: is the feature you have just come to the one marked on the map? In short, is it mapworthy? Let me explain what I mean with the help of some examples.

The ground can look very different after heavy rain. A fold that is normally dry can have a stream rushing down it only to be dry again a few hours later. It is easy to mistake one of these for a stream marked on the map. Ask yourself how far have I gone since my last positive marker? How far is the stream on the map from that point? That may give you the answer immediately. If it does not, check its direction or the direction and gradient of the slopes on either side. It must all fit.

Now try an example using the map extract overleaf. You are at the car park (SU 791 181) south west of Harting Downs and plan to walk in an easterly direction along the South Downs Way. From the map, what features on the ground might you expect to see on the way to Beacon Hill and beyond? Moving off along the path, to the north you will be aware of the steep escarpment dropping away from you. About 800 metres out from the car park you will pass into non-coniferous woodland, 300 metres further on you will cross a bridleway and start to climb steeply towards Beacon Hill (SU 807 184). As you pass Beacon Hill you may well see signs of the ramparts of an ancient fort. Passing by the hill your path will cross another bridleway at SU 809 184 which runs north east down the escarpment. After crossing this bridleway you will be travelling due east for a distance of about 300 metres parallel with the edge of mixed woodland 100 metres to your north.

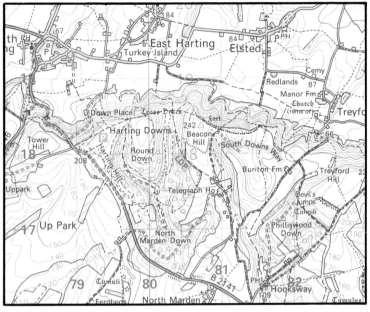

OS Landranger 197

Occasionally you may be puzzled to come across a feature that does not appear to be marked on the map or perhaps a feature marked on the map does not appear to be there on the ground. First ask yourself: is it the shape of the ground or a feature on the surface? If it is the shape it is a certainty that you are wrong and not the map.

The shape of the land, and the flow of the streams and rivers that made it that way, has changed very little over the years since maps were first made. It is man who has changed the environment. If it is something on the surface, assess how long ago it was created. Are the trees newly planted? Has a wood been felled and turned into fields? Look for new fencing and newly cut ditches with no weeds. Is the road, track or housing estate new? Have old buildings been recently demolished?

Next, compare your assessment with the date of the latest information on the map. But be careful. The date of the latest information is not necessarily the date the map was printed. In the legend of the map there will be either a statement or a small diagram, sometimes both, showing the date of the information on the map and the date the map was printed. Do not confuse the two. The date of the latest information is the more important piece of information for the map-reader. Note that the date of the latest information can vary in different parts of the map and according to the type of feature. New roads are often more up to date than other information on the map. Here is an example of how this information is displayed on an Ordnance Survey map:

COMPILATION AND REVISION

Base map constructed on Transverse Mercator Projection, Airy Spheroid, OSGB (1936) Datum
Vertical datum mean sea level (Newlyn)

Low water mark plotted from air photographs dated 1962-80
Revised 1985
Major roads revised 1986

Derivation of contours

1   From contours surveyed at 1:10 000 scale and 10m vertical interval
2   By interpolation from contours surveyed at 1:10 560 scale and 25ft
    vertical interval
3   From one inch to one mile seventh series maps

1

Contour values in lakes are in metres

A booklet, "Place names on maps of Scotland and Wales", is published by the Ordnance Survey, and includes a glossary of the most common Gaelic, Scandinavian and Welsh elements used on Ordnance Survey maps of Scotland and Wales

---

OS Landranger 55

BEFORE YOU START

There is one other rule that is so obvious that I hesitate to mention it. Yet I have seen what should have been enjoyable hikes ruined and military operations come to a halt through failure to observe it.

MAKE SURE YOU HAVE THE RIGHT MAPS

There is nothing more embarassing, and sometimes alarming, than to reach the edge of a map sheet, take out what you think is the adjoining sheet and find it is the wrong one. Do check all map sheets before you start.

Clearly, you must choose the right scale of map for your purpose. For the motorist a scale of 1:250 000, or sometimes even smaller, is usually adequate to get from town to town. But it can be helpful to have a larger scale map of the area around your destination. For the walker and motorist off the beaten track 1:50,000 or larger is ideal.

If your route takes you near the edge of a map sheet, even if you do not intend to go off it, it is always wise to take the next sheet as well. You can never tell when bad weather or an accident might force you to change course on to a neighbouring map sheet. It happens more often than you might think, so be prepared.

Never assume you have got the right map sheets. Look at them and check, not only that they are the right ones but also that they are serviceable and are not worn into holes at the corners of the folds. It helps if you slip the one you are using into a polythene bag to protect it. Try and find thicker-than-usual polythene as it lasts so much longer. Bags that hardware shops use for nails are the best.

Next check that your compass is in good working order, particularly if you had a fall, accidentally trod on it or left it too near a metal object in storage or during your last outing. Also, be warned that some types of insect repellent can cause plastic to craze over so that it is almost impossible to see through. This includes watch 'glass'. Do not forget to check the lanyard for strength.

Planning Your Route

For the keen map reader, planning your route is a major part of the fun of travelling. There is an old military adage that time spent in reconnaissance is seldom wasted. It applies just as much to time spent studying a map of the ground as it does to studying the ground itself. The route you look for will depend on why you are making the journey. For some it will be to admire the view from a scenic route, others will be seeking out the rocky ground and cliffs to go climbing. I will not insult your intelligence by listing the factors you will take into account in making your choice. However, I do suggest if you are having problems making a choice that you ask yourself What is the purpose of my journey? Only a good knowledge of map-reading backed by experience can teach you how to select the best route.

Spend some time before your trip studying the map. You can do it at leisure the evening beforehand, in the train or car on the way to your start point or even at the start point. The important thing is to do it. Do not just look at the map blankly. You have to use your brain. First, form a general picture of the lie of the land in your mind's eye. The major features: hills, valleys, roads and villages. Choose a possible route. Then make a mental journey along it picturing what you are likely to see on either side. Look particularly for places where the going will be difficult: marsh, rivers, scree, cliffs or even woods. They are all marked on the map so there can be no excuses if you come upon them unexpectedly.

Remember that ridges are easier to follow than rivers unless they have a towpath along them. Use the public footpaths and other marked public rights of way. If you do not like what you find, repeat the process until you make a satisfactory choice.

Be sure to look at the date of the latest information on the map. This will help if you encounter the unexpected and save you having to unfold the map to check the date if you do. Besides, why risk spoiling a journey by using an out-of-date map?

If you do decide to buy a new map, be sure to check by looking carefully in the margins the date of the latest information before you make your purchase, especially in the case of foreign maps. It is also better to go if you can to a specialist map shop where you can obtain the latest editions, although any map is better than no map!

Not Quite Sure

I was tempted to subtitle this paragraph The Map Must Be Wrong. I did not, because it never is. At worst it may be out of date. If you find yourself in the unhappy position of realising that the ground you are on does not fit where you think you are on the map, first give yourself a mental ticking off for not sticking to the four rules, then stop at once. There is nothing worse than ploughing on, hoping that it will all come right round the next bend. It will not, and you will only end up further off course with a longer march to get back on it.

There is a great temptation to bend the rules to fit what you find. The scenario goes something like this: "Funny, we seem to have got to the top of the hill after only two hundred metres. It should have been about 400. Oh, well, I expect it was. Ah, there's the track I was expecting. Good. If we hurry we'll get to the pub before it shuts. Pity the mist is obscuring the view, but let's push on." Two hours later you are still trying to find your way to the pub, not for a drink, but to make certain you are back on route. What happened? You were not at the top of the hill. It was obscured by mist. That track which you jumped to the conclusion was the one you wanted, was one made by sheep and not marked on the map. It went off down a spur running parallel to the main ridge for the first few hundred metres then veered off at right angles. Did you check its direction before setting off along it, and again when it changed course? No you did not. Although you remembered the scale, you did not trust its accuracy.

I will say it again: Everything must fit. If you are uncertain where you are, stop, get your compass out, check the direction and distance to at least three recognisable features that will be marked on the map then study the map until you find a spot where they are all in exactly the right place. Do not just rely on one fix in difficult map-reading conditions, check in three or four directions. If you are a beginner get into the habit right from the start on the easy routes. To me the fun of map-reading is spotting how all the features marked on the map are where they should be on the ground. It makes one appreciate the skill of the map maker and just how much information there is on a map.

Still puzzled? Unable to find a spot where they all fit? Then look back at the features you used to try and check your position. Is the church you can see the one you are looking at on the map? Has it got a spire or a tower? The one on the map has a spire just like the one on the ground but the map shows some houses 200 metres directly to the west, has the one on the ground? No! Then it cannot be the right one. Look at the next village along the valley. Ah, that has a church with a spire that stands on its own and there is a wood 400 metres to the south, just like the one I can see. Getting warmer, now let's see if all the other points fit …

Your mental attitude needs to be like that of a good detective who can not just ignore any evidence that does not fit his theory but has to continue investigating until all the clues fit the jigsaw.

Still stuck? Then go back to the last position you were 100% certain was correct. If necessary go right back to check that you are 100% certain where you started from. Then work forward again from there.

To summarise, the simplest way to find your position on a map is:

1. Set the map.
2. Establish the distance and direction to three prominent points on the ground.
3. Remember the scale.
4. Identify on the map the points you found on the ground.
5. Work out your position.

SPECIAL SITUATIONS

AT NIGHT

The obvious point about travel on foot by night across country is that you do not do it unless you have to. It is more difficult, slower and occasionally dangerous. However for the benefit of those of you forced to travel by night here are some tips that may help you keep to your route.

If you can, beforehand in daylight, have a good look at the countryside you are going to have to cross. Memorise the key features. Choose a route that makes maximum use of paths, hedgerows, fences, ridgelines, edges of woods or anything that will help you maintain direction. It is better to choose a slightly longer route where the going is easy and you have a clearly visible marker to help you stay on course than it is to plough directly across country on a compass bearing. Keep away from rivers, lakes and ponds; they have streams and ditches that run into them which are very wet when you fall into them in the dark. Footbridges can be hard to spot at night.

Memorise the route beforehand. Try not to use a torch to read the map as it destroys night vision. If you have to, try to use one eye only. Although the eyes work as a pair you will find that the one you keep closed regains its night vision much quicker than the one subjected to the bright light of the torch.

Move slowly and quietly. You may be lucky and see some unexpected wildlife. Your sense of hearing will be more acute than it is by day and the sound of a vehicle on a road or a dog barking at a farm can give useful confirmation that you are on course. Finally, be sure to take safety precautions if you are moving on roads or country lanes at night. The key points to remember are:

1. Wear a reflective jacket, cross-belt or arm band.
2. Walk on the side facing the oncoming traffic.
3. Cross motorways and railways only by bridges or underpasses.
4. Keep to the pavement if there is one.
5. Step off the road if you see or hear traffic approaching.
6. If you belong to an organised body, obey its rules.

LEADING A PARTY

Before leading a party you must be experienced and trained in specific skills. There are various organisations that can help you in this respect, some of which are listed on pages 47 and 48. One of the most important requirements of a party leader is that they know where they are going. That means consistently accurate map-reading. When asked by a member of the party where they are, always be as accurate as possible in giving your position rather than jabbing at the map with a finger and saying "somewhere around here". A fingertip covers a distance of 400 metres at 1:50000 scale! Giving an accurate position will maintain confidence in your leadership ability.

The next most important thing a leader should do is to keep the party informed of progress. Give them an outline of the route before you start and keep them informed as you go along. It helps to boost confidence in your ability when it all turns out as predicted. "Three more streams and two more ridges to cross before we hit the road. We should do it in a couple of hours," is much better for morale than "Another six miles to go." The members of the party can count the ridges and ration their energy accordingly. If at any time you decide to change your plans, let them know immediately. There is nothing worse than an inexplicable change of course if you are tail-end Charlie struggling to keep up at the back.

- **Remember the person at the back**. No one likes being last but someone has to be. Rather than let it be one of the weaker members of the party who continually has to struggle to keep up, it is better to ask one of the stronger, more responsible members of the party to bring up the rear. The task can be rotated if necessary.

- **Avoid 'bunching' at obstacles**. If you are leading a party strung out over a distance of 50 metres and you come to an obstacle that slows you down such as a stile, then you must continue at the same speed at which you cross the obstacle for the next 50 metres and then increase speed gradually after that until you are back at normal pace. If you do not, you will soon find that the party has got strung out over a much greater distance and those at the back are having difficulty in keeping up.

- **Develop a drill for halts so that everyone knows and understands the routine**. It does not matter too much what it is so long as it is known and followed. It helps to avoid bickering and misunderstandings particularly at the end of the day when people are getting tired. If you are with a group that has not been out together before, take a couple of minutes before you move off to explain how you like it done. It will pay dividends by welding what could become a disorganised rabble into a cohesive party. Your explanation should cover:

Frequency of halts. Ten minutes in every hour is usual. It allows time to take boots off to attend to blisters, adjust equipment or get something out of a pack.

Signal for halts. You need to give a clear signal that it is a proper halt and not just a pause while you check your map, otherwise you can find those behind have sat down or taken off their packs.

Type of halt. Your signal should make it clear whether you want the party to close up in a bunch or stop where they are, strung out behind you. If they are to close up, you should time the halt from the moment the last person gets in, not from when the leader stops. Clearly you are not going to close up if you are strung out along a narrow track leading up the side of an escarpment, it would merely waste time. However if you have reached the summit of a hill then you will want to close everyone up so they can all enjoy the view.

FIXING A RENDEZVOUS POINT

For two or more parties to meet is a task which sounds easy yet is one which, if instructions are not absolutely clear, can give rise to horrible muddle, confusion and delay. The simplest and most accurate method is to give a grid reference and time, there can be no doubt about that.

"We'll meet by the river at SJ 687030 at 1400 hrs." What could be clearer than that? Well, they met alright. The trouble was that one party was on the north bank and the other on the south with the river running 50 feet below them in a 10 metre wide ravine with no way across. It took an hour to reunite them. If there is any room for doubt, be specific.

It is wise to make sure your instructions cover what to do if one party fails to arrive at the appointed time. Injuries can occur, people can get delayed for many reasons. How long to wait and what should be done next must be covered.

IN A VEHICLE

The same rules apply for map-reading in a vehicle as for map-reading on foot. Knowing where you start is usually less of a problem in a vehicle and checking direction is less important so long as you start down the right road. Remembering the scale is still very important but checking how far you have gone is made much easier by the trip recorder or odometer on the vehicle. The main difference is that things happen so much more quickly that it is even more important to read ahead and anticipate what is coming next.

It is a nuisance if you have to stop to look at a map en route. There never seems to be a suitable spot at the moment you decide to check. To avoid this, some drivers like to write the route on a slip of paper and fasten it to the dashboard or sun visor. This is certainly one way of doing it and it is better than placing it on the passenger seat beside you. A simple way of recording a route is shown below.

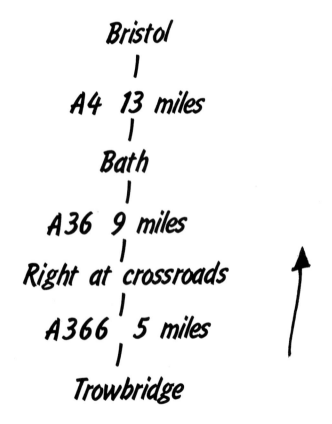

Bristol
|
A4 13 miles
|
Bath
|
A36 9 miles
|
Right at crossroads
|
A366 5 miles
|
Trowbridge

When planning your route, it is helpful to know that on Ordnance Survey road maps, selected places of major traffic importance (known officially as primary route destinations) are shown with a green background on the map. The same towns are named on the green-backed road signs. So look for these towns when planning.

When reading ahead go for features that cross your route: bridges over or under railway lines and rivers, level crossings and power lines, or prominent features like churches and major road junctions.

Keep the map set so that things appear on the proper side of the road. You can read the odd place name upside down but not a map.

The last 200m is always the most difficult. For this it is best to resort to a town plan if you have one. If you are taking telephoned instructions on how to find your destination from the person you are visiting, it is wise to follow the route on a large scale map beside you as they talk. Some people have very strange ideas of distance and direction!

Finally, if there are two of you, the navigator/passenger concentrates on the map while the driver concentrates on the road. The driver should call out the names of places, roads or prominent features as they are passed while the navigator keeps track of the route on the map. If you are navigating and do look up, make sure you keep your finger on the map at the last spot you identified. On a bumpy road you may have travelled a couple of hundred metres before you can find the spot again.

FOREIGN MAPS

Although different in design and content and often less detailed than Ordnance Survey maps, foreign maps follow similar principles and conventions in their use of scale, signs and colour to depict landscape habitation and communications in plan form. The basic map-reading rules in this book therefore still apply.

AUTOROUTES	MOTORWAYS		AUTOBAHNEN
Autoroute, point de jonction, nom de la sortie	Motorway, junctions, name of the exit		Autobahn, Anschlußstelle, Ausfahrtsname
Aire de service , péage	Service area, t oll		Service-Center ,Gebühr
Aire de repos, poste d'essence	Lay by, filling station		Raststätte, Tankstelle
Restaurant, hôtel	Restaurant, hotel		Restaurant, Hotel
Kilométrage ❶ global ❷ partiel	Kilometre-distance ❶ in total ❷ partial		Entfernungsangaben ❶ Fernkilometer ❷ Nahkilometer
Autoroute ❶ en construction ❷ en projet	Motorway ❶ under construction ❷ projected		Autobahn ❶ im Bau ❷ in Planung

ROUTES	ROADS		STRAßEN
Route à chaussées indépendantes	Dual carriageways		Zweibahnige Schnellstraße
Route à quatre voies	Four carriageways		Vierspurige Schnellstraße
Grand itinéraire	Primary route		Fernverkehrsstraße
Route à grande circulation	High traffic road		Hauptverkehrsstraße
Hauteur limitée Limite de charge en tonnes	Limited headroom Load limit in T.		Zulässige Gesamthöhe Höchstbelastung in T.
Route recommandée ou liaison principale	Recommended route or principal connection		Wichtige Verbindungsstraße
Autres routes	Other roads		Sonstige Straße
Route de viabilité incertaine, sentier	Road of incertain viability, path		Straße von zweifelhafter Befahrbarkeit, Fußweg
Route forestière	Forest road		Forststraße
Route pittoresque	Picturesque road		Landschaftlich schöne Straße
Route en construction	Road under construction		Straße im Bau
Route en projet	Route projected		Straße in planung
Col, altitude	Pass, Height		Paß, Höhenangabe
Montée (sens de la flèche) 10 % et plus	Steep hill (direction of the arrow) 10 % and more		Steigung (in Pfeilrichtung) 10 % und mehr
Col fermé en période d'enneigement	Pass closed at periods of snowfall		Paß, während der Schneeperiode geschlossen
Route interdite	Prohibited road		Gesperrte Straße
Kilométrage ❶ global ❷ partiel	Kilometre-distance ❶ in total ❷ partial		Entfernungsangaben ❶ Fernkilometer ❷ Nahkilometer

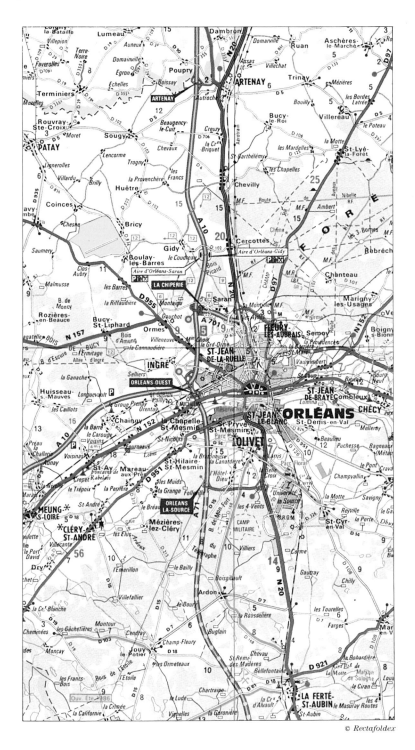

45

THE COUNTRY CODE

When you are on your way, The Countryside Commission urges you to keep to these points of the Country Code:

* Guard against all risk of fire.

* Take your litter home.

* Keep to public paths across farmland.

* Use gates and stiles to cross fences, hedges and walls.

* Fasten all gates after you.

* Protect wildlife, plants and trees.

* Make no unnecessary noise.

CONVERSION TABLE

Imperial	*Metric*
1 inch	25.40 millimetres
1 foot	30.48 centimetres
1 yard	0.9144 metres
1 mile	1.609 kilometres
1 sq. inch	6.4516 sq. centimetres
1 sq. foot	0.0929 sq. metres
1 sq. yard	0.8361 sq. metres
1 sq. mile	2.5899 sq. kilometres
1 acre (4840 sq. yards)	0.4047 hectares

Metric	Imperial
1 millimetre	0.0394 inches
1 centimetre	0.394 inches
1 metre	3.281 feet
1 kilometre	0.621 miles
1 sq. centimetre	0.155 sq. inches
1 sq. metre	10.7639 sq. feet
	1.1959 sq. yards
1 sq. kilometre	0.3861 sq. miles
1 hectare (10,000 sq. metres)	2.471 acres

Imperial	Metric	Metric	Imperial
1 pint	0.5683 litres	1 litre	0.220 gallons
1 gallon	4.546 litres		

USEFUL ADDRESSES

Ramblers Association
1-5 Wandsworth Road
London SW8
Tel: 01 582 6826

Countryside Commission
John Dower House
Crescent Place
Cheltenham, Gloucestershire GL50 3RA
Tel: 0242 521381

The Scout Association
Baden-Powell House, 65 Queen's Gate
London SW7
Tel: 01 5584 7030

Girl Guides Association
17 Buckingham Palace Road
London SW1
Tel: 01 834 6242

Silva (UK) Ltd Compasses.
15 Bolney Way
Feltham Middlesex TW13 6DB
Tel: 01 898 6901

Ordnance Survey
Information Enquiries
Ordnance Survey
Romsey Road
Maybush
Southampton, Hampshire SO9 4DH
Tel: 0703 792763 or 792749

Main Agents
England and Wales
The London Map Centre
22-24 Caxton Street
London SW1
Tel: 01 222 2466/7

Scotland
Thomas Nelson & Sons Ltd
51 York Place
Edinburgh
Tel: 031 557 3011

Automobile Association
Head Office: Fanum House
Basingstoke
Hampshire RG21 2EA
Tel: 0256 20213

Royal Automobile Club
P.O. Box 100
Lansdowne Road
Croydon CR9 2JA
Tel: 01 686 2525

Cyclists' Touring Club
69 Meadrow
Godalming, Surrey GU7 3HS
Tel: 048 68 7217

Mountain Walking Leader Training Scheme
Crawford House
Precinct Centre
Booth Street East
Manchester M13 NR2
Tel: 061 273 5839

Duke of Edinburgh's Award Scheme
5 Prince of Wales Terrace   London W8
Tel: 01 937 5205